any h   ch of

SNAPPED BY SAM

Level 5A

Written by Melanie Hamm
Illustrated by Emmeline Pidgen

What is synthetic phonics?

Synthetic phonics teaches children to recognise the sounds of letters and to blend (synthesise) them together to make whole words.

Understanding sound/letter relationships gives children the confidence and ability to read unfamiliar words, without having to rely on memory or guesswork; this helps them to progress towards independent reading.

Did you know? Spoken English uses more than 40 speech sounds. Each sound is called a *phoneme*. Some phonemes relate to a single letter (d-o-g) and others to combinations of letters (sh-ar-p). When a phoneme is written down it is called a *grapheme*. Teaching these sounds, matching them to their written form and sounding out words for reading is the basis of synthetic phonics.

Consultant

I love reading phonics has been created in consultation with language expert Abigail Steel. She has a background in teaching and teacher training and is a respected expert in the field of synthetic phonics. Abigail Steel is a regular contributor to educational publications. Her international education consultancy supports parents and teachers in the promotion of literacy skills.

Reading tips

 This book focuses on the t sound, made with the letters ed, as in tripped.

Tricky words in this book

Any words in bold may have unusual spellings or are new and have not yet been introduced.

> Tricky words in this book:
>
> ## fence picture

Extra ways to have fun with this book

After the reader has read the story, ask them questions about what they have just read:

What things did Sam snap that annoyed his friends?
Which picture did you think was the best?

What would you snap?

A pronunciation guide

This grid contains the sounds used in the stories in levels 4, 5 and 6 and a guide on how to say them. /a/ represents the sounds made, rather than the letters in a word.

/ai/ as in game	/ai/ as in play/they	/ee/ as in leaf/these	/ee/ as in he
/igh/ as in kite/light	/igh/ as in find/sky	/oa/ as in home	/oa/ as in snow
/oa/ as in cold	/y+oo/ as in cube/music/new	long /oo/ as in flute/crew/blue	/oi/ as in boy
/er/ as in bird/hurt	/or/ as in snore/oar/door	/or/ as in dawn/sauce/walk	/e/ as in head
/e/ as in said/any	/ou/ as in cow	/u/ as in touch	/air/ as in hare/bear/there
/eer/ as in deer/here/cashier	/t/ as in tripped/skipped	/d/ as in rained	/j/ as in gent/gin/gym
/j/ as in barge/hedge	/s/ as in cent/circus/cyst	/s/ as in prince	/s/ as in house
/ch/ as in itch/catch	/w/ as in white	/h/ as in who	/r/ as in write/rhino

Sounds in this story are
highlighted in the grid.

/**f**/ as in phone	/**f**/ as in rough	/**ul**/ as in pencil/ hospital	/**z**/ as in fries/ cheese/breeze
/**n**/ as in knot/ gnome/engine	/**m**/ as in welcome /thumb/column	/**g**/ as in guitar/ghost	/**zh**/ as in vision/beige
/**k**/ as in chord	/**k**/ as in plaque/ bouquet	/**nk**/ as in uncle	/**ks**/ as in box/books/ ducks/cakes
/**a**/ and /**o**/ as in hat/what	/**e**/ and /**ee**/ as in bed/he	/**i**/ and /**igh**/ as in fin/find	/**o**/ and /**oa**/ as in hot/cold
/**u**/ and short /**oo**/ as in but/put	/**ee**/, /**e**/ and /**ai**/ as in eat/ bread/break	/**igh**/, /**ee**/ and /**e**/ as in tie/field/friend	/**ou**/ and /**oa**/ as in cow/blow
/**ou**/, /**oa**/ and /**oo**/ as in out/ shoulder/could	/**i**/ and /**ai**/ as in money/they	/**c**/ and /**s**/ as in cat/cent	/**y**/, /**igh**/ and /**i**/ as in yes/sky/myth
/**g**/ and /**j**/ as in got/giant	/**ch**/, /**c**/ and /**sh**/ as in chin/ school/chef	/**er**/, /**air**/ and /**eer**/ as in earth/bear/ears	/**u**/, /**ou**/ and /**oa**/ as in plough/dough

Be careful not to add an 'uh' sound to 's', 't', 'p',
'c', 'h', 'r', 'm', 'd', 'g', 'l', 'f' and 'b'. For example,
say 'fff' not 'fuh' and 'sss' not 'suh'.

Sam had a new camera.
He snapped everything he saw.

He snapped the birds as they
flapped and the dogs as
they yapped.

Sam snapped Sally as she
skipped. She did not mind.

He snapped Chaz as he shopped.
He did not mind.

But then Sam snapped Ben as
he tripped. Ben was fed up!

11

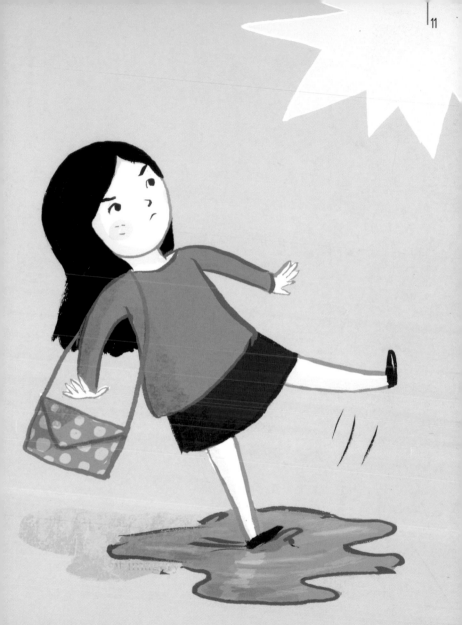

Next Sam snapped Jo as she
slipped. Jo was angry!

Sam snapped Billy as he flopped
and napped.

Billy woke and was cross.

Then Sam saw a horse as it
clip-clopped down the lane.

He stepped on the **fence** to get
near. But he slipped off!

Sam dropped into a hole. He was trapped!

Ben, Jo and Billy stopped by.
Were they still cross?

No! They threw Sam a rope and he gripped it.

They helped him up from
the hole.

Sam was saved and everybody clapped.

Up popped Tim. He snapped the rescue with his camera.

Ben, Jo, Billy and Sam looked at the **picture**.

It was good! Now Sam just
snaps if everybody is happy!

OVER **48** TITLES IN SIX LEVELS
Abigail Steel recommends...

Some titles from Level 4

The Maze
978-1-84898-559-9

Fairy Fay's Bad Day
978-1-84898-560-5

Pirate School
978-1-84898-566-7

Other titles to enjoy from Level 5

Max's Trip
978-1-84898-562-9

George the Genius Gerbil
978-1-84898-567-4

Budge Troll, Budge!
978-1-84898-568-1

Some titles from Level 6

What Wally Wanted
978-1-84898-563-6

Superhero Ed
978-1-84898-564-3

The Robot Bop
978-1-84898-570-4

An Hachette UK Company
www.hachette.co.uk

Copyright © Octopus Publishing Group Ltd 2012
First published in Great Britain in 2012 by TickTock, an imprint of Octopus Publishing Group Ltd,
Endeavour House, 189 Shaftesbury Avenue, London WC2H 8JY.
www.octopusbooks.co.uk

ISBN 978 1 84898 561 2

Printed and bound in China
10 9 8 7 6 5 4 3 2 1